IGOR
STRAVINSKY

PETRUSHKA

IN FULL SCORE

ORIGINAL VERSION

Dover Publications, Inc., New York

Александръ Бенуа

[TO ALEXANDRE BENOIS]

Copyright © 1988 by Dover Publications, Inc.
All rights reserved under Pan American and International Copyright Conventions.

Published in Canada by General Publishing Company, Ltd., 30 Lesmill Road, Don Mills, Toronto, Ontario.
Published in the United Kingdom by Constable and Company, Ltd.

This Dover edition, first published in 1988, is a republication of *Pétrouchka (Scènes Burlesques en 4 Tableaux d'Igor Stravinsky et Alexandre Benois): Partition d'Orchestre*, originally published by Edition Russe de Musique / Russischer Musikverlag, Berlin, Moscow, St. Petersburg, in 1912. The French stage directions have been replaced by English translations (but the French—corrected—appears in the new table of contents). The French listing of the personnel of the premiere is incorporated into the new English version of that list. An English translation of the introductory texts replaces the French and Russian versions, an English list of instruments has been added, and a new table of contents has been prepared.
We are grateful to the Northwestern University Library for the loan of its score.

Manufactured in the United States of America
Dover Publications, Inc., 31 East 2nd Street, Mineola, N.Y. 11501

Library of Congress Cataloging-in-Publication Data

Stravinsky, Igor, 1882–1971.
  Petrushka : in full score : original version.

  Ballet.
  Reprint. Originally published: Pétrouchka. Berlin : Edition russe de musique ; New York : Breitkopf & Härtel, 1912. With introductory matter translated into English.
  1. Ballets—Scores.   I. Title.
M1520.S9P3   1988   88-750374
ISBN 0-486-25680-4

CONTENTS

Igor Stravinsky
PETRUSHKA

Burlesque Scenes in 4 Tableaux
by Igor Stravinsky and Alexandre Benois

PETRUSHKA

Premiere Performance at the Théâtre du Châtelet
(Paris, 13 June 1911)

Under the Management of
SERGE DE DIAGHILEV

Artistic director: Alexandre Benois. Choreographic director: Michel Fokine.

Characters	Cast
The Ballerina [La Ballerine]	Tamara Karsavina
Petrushka [Pétrouchka]	Vaslav Nijinsky
The Moor [Le Maure]	Aleksandr Orlov
The Old Magician [Le vieux Charlatan]	Enrico Cecchetti

The Wet-Nurses [Les Nourrices (Nounous)]: Baranovich I, Baranovich II, A. Vasilieva, M. Vasilieva, Gachevska, Tchernycheva, Lastchilina, Sazonova, Biber.

The Coachmen [Les Cochers]: Lastchilin, Semënov, Petrov, V. Romanov, Orlik.

The Grooms [Les Palefreniers]: Rosaï, A. Molotsov.

The Reveling Merchant [Le Marchand fêtard]: Koussov.

The Gypsy Women [Les tziganes]: Schollar, Reisen.

The Street Dancers [Les danseuses de rue]: Bronislava Nijinska, Vassilievska.

First Organ-Grinder [Premier joueur d'orgue]: Sergheiev.

Second Organ-Grinder [Second joueur d'orgue]: Kobelev.

The "Died" (master of ceremonies) [Le "Died" (compère de la foire)]: Romanov.

The Peepshow Exhibitor [Le montreur de vues d'optique]: Ognev.

Mummers and maskers [Masques et travestis]: Larionova, Kandina; Leontiev, Kremniev, Ulanov, S. Molotsov, Dmitriev, Gouduin, Kotchetovsky, Masslov, Gerassimov, Christapson, Larosov.

Shopkeepers (male and female) [marchands, marchandes], Officers [officiers], Soldiers [soldats], Noblemen [seigneurs], Ladies [dames], Children [enfants], Housemaids [bonnes], Cossacks [cosaques], Policemen [agents de la police], A Bear-Tamer [un montreur d'ours], etc.

Conductor: Pierre Monteux
Scenes and dances choreographed and directed by Michel Fokine

Sets and costumes designed by Alexandre Benois

Sets built by Boris Anisfeld

Costumes sewn by Caffi and Vorobiev

GENERAL NOTE

The action takes place in St. Petersburg, in Admiralty Square, around 1830. In addition to the ordinary curtain, there is a special curtain for the "burlesque scenes." This curtain represents the Magician, grandiosely portrayed, enthroned on the clouds. The ordinary curtain rises when the music begins and falls at the end of the show. The special curtain rises a bit later and falls between the tableaux.*

I. A sunny winter day. At the left, a large booth with a balcony for the "Died" (master of ceremonies). Beneath it, a table with a gigantic samovar. In the middle of the set, the Magician's little theater; at right, stalls selling sweets and a peepshow. At the rear can be seen merry-go-rounds, swings, and slides. A crowd of strollers onstage, including common people, gentlemen and ladies, groups of drunkards arm in arm; children surrounding the peepshow; women crowding around the stalls.

II. Petrushka's cell. Its cardboard walls are painted black, with stars and a half-moon. Figures of devils on a gold background decorate the leaves of the folding doors that lead into the Ballerina's room. On one of the cell's walls, the portrait of the scowling Magician (a bit below and to the side is where Petrushka punches a hole in his fit of despair).

III. The Moor's cell. Wallpaper with a pattern of green palms and fantastic fruits on a red background. The Moor, in a costume of great splendor, is lying on a very low sofa and playing with a coconut. To the right, the door that leads to the Ballerina's cell.

IV. The same set as in the 1st tableau. Toward the end, an effect of late evening. At the entrance of the mummers, Bengal lights are lit in the wings. At the moment of Petrushka's death it begins to snow and the darkness deepens.

---

*There are precise indications in the score for raising and lowering the two curtains.

"PETRUSHKA"

(Burlesque Scenes in 4 Tableaux)

In the midst of the Shrovetide festivities, an old Magician of oriental appearance exhibits before an astonished crowd the animated puppets Petrushka, the Ballerina, and the Moor, who perform a wild dance.

The Magician's magic has endowed them with all the human feelings and passions. Petrushka has been given more than the others. Therefore he suffers more than the Ballerina and the Moor. He resents bitterly the cruelty of the Magician, his bondage, his exclusion from ordinary life, his ugliness, and his ridiculous appearance. He seeks comfort in the love of the Ballerina, and is on the point of believing in his success. But the lovely one shuns him, feeling only terror at his bizarre behavior.

The Moor's life is completely different. He is brutish and wicked, but his splendid appearance fascinates the Ballerina, who tries to seduce him using all her charms and finally succeeds. Just at the moment of the love scene, Petrushka appears, enraged with jealousy, but the Moor quickly throws him out the door.

The Shrovetide fair is at its height. A reveling merchant accompanied by gypsy singers throws handfuls of bank notes to the crowd. Coachmen dance with wet-nurses, a bear-tamer appears with his beast, and finally a band of mummers sweeps everyone up in a diabolical melee. All at once cries are heard from the Magician's little theater. The rivalry between the Moor and Petrushka finally takes a tragic turn. The animated puppets dash from the theater, and the Moor knocks Petrushka down with a blow of his saber. The wretched Petrushka dies in the snow, surrounded by the holiday crowd. The Magician, whom a policeman has gone to fetch, hastens to reassure everyone, and in his hands Petrushka becomes a puppet again. He invites the crowd to verify that the head is wooden and the body is filled with bran. The crowd disperses. The Magician, now alone, catches sight, to his great terror, of Petrushka's ghost above the little theater, menacing him and making mocking gestures at all whom the Magician has fooled.

INSTRUMENTATION

2 Flauti piccoli { (Fl. picc. I — poi Fl. gr. IV) (Fl. picc. II — poi Fl. gr. III)	2 Piccolos { (Picc. I = Fl. IV) (Picc. II = Fl. III)
2 Flauti grandi	2 Flutes
4 Oboi (Ob. IV — poi Corno Inglese)	4 Oboes (Ob. IV = English Horn)
3 Clarinetti in Si♭ (poi in La)	3 Clarinets (B♭, A)
Clarinetto basso in Si♭ (poi clar. IV)	Bass Clarinet (B♭) (= Cl. IV)
3 Fagotti	3 Bassoons
Contrafagotto (poi Fag. IV)	Contrabassoon (= Bsn. IV)
4 Corni in F	4 Horns (F)
2 Pistoni in Si♭ (poi in La)	2 Cornets (B♭, A)
2 Trombe in Si♭ (poi in La, poi Tromba I = Tr. picc. in Re)	2 Trumpets (B♭, A) (Tr. I = D Trumpet)
3 Tromboni	3 Trombones
Tuba	Tuba
Timpani	Timpani
Cassa	Bass Drum
Piatti	Cymbals
Tamtam	Tam-tam
Triangolo	Triangle
Tambour de Basque*)	Tambourine*
Tambour militaire Tambour de Provence (Tambourin) } Dans la coulisse	Side Drum Long Drum } offstage
Campanelli (est écrit une 8ve au dessous)	Glockenspiel (notated an 8ve below concert pitch)
Celesta à 2 et à 4 mains (est écrit une 8ve au dessous)	Celesta (for 2 and 4 hands) (notated an 8ve below concert pitch)
Piano	Piano
2 Harpes	2 Harps
Xylophone (est écrit à la hauteur réelle)	Xylophone (notated at concert pitch)
Quintuor à corde	Strings

---

*) ♪ = secouer l'instrument.   𝆮 = frotter avec le pouce.

NB. Pour les instruments de cuivre se servir des sourdines en cuivre.

* ♪ = shake the instrument.   𝆮 = rub with the thumb.

NB: For the brass instruments, use metal mutes.

КАРТИНА ПЕРВАЯ.
НАРОДНЫЯ ГУЛЯНІЯ НА МАСЛЕНОИ.

FIRST TABLEAU
The Shrovetide Fair.

ПРОХОДИТЪ, ПРИПЛЯСЫВАЯ, НЕБОЛЬШАЯ ТОЛПА ПОДПИВШИХЪ ГУЛЯКЪ.
A Group of Drunken Revelers Passes, Dancing.

ВЫСОТЫ СВОЕГО БАЛАГАНА ПОТѢШАЕТЪ ТОЛПУ.
Entertains the Crowd from His Booth Above.

ВЪ ТОЛПѢ ПОЯВЛЯЕТСЯ ШАРМАНЩИКЪ СЪ УЛИЧНОЙ ТАНЦОВЩИЦЕЙ.
An Organ-Grinder Appears in the Crowd with a [Woman] Dancer.

22

13 УЛИЧНАЯ ТАНЦОВЩИЦА ТАНЦУЕТЪ, ОТБИВАЯ ТАКТЪ ТРЕУГОЛЬНИКОМЪ.
The Dancer Dances, Beating Time on the Triangle.

*)ШАРМАНЩИКЪ, ПРОДОЛЖАЯ ОДНОЙ РУКОЙ ВЕРТѢТЬ ШАРМАНКУ, ДРУГОЮ ИГРАЕТЪ НА КОРНЕТЪ - А - 14 ПИСТОНѢ
The Organ-Grinder, Continuing to Turn the Crank with One Hand, Plays the Cornet with the Other.

НА ДРУГОМЪ КОНЦѢ СЦЕНЫ ИГРАЕТЪ ЯЩИКЪ СЪ МУЗЫКОЙ,
At the Other End of the Stage a Music Box Plays, Another [Woman]

ВОКРУГЪ КОТОРАГО ТАНЦУЕТЪ ДРУГАЯ УЛИЧНАЯ ТАНЦОВЩИЦА.
Dancer Dancing Around It.

ПЕРВАЯ ТАНЦОВЩИ-
The First Dancer Plays

-ЦА СНОВА БЬЕТЪ ВЪ ТРЕУГОЛЬНИКЪ.
the Triangle Again.

ВОЗВРАЩАЕТСЯ ВЕСЕЛАЯ КАМПАНІЯ ГУЛЯКЪ.
The Merry Group Returns.

34

ВЛЕКАЮТЪ ВНИМАНІЕ ТОЛПЫ БАРАБАННЫМЪ БОЕМЪ.
Attract the Attention of the Crowd by Their Drumrolls.

ИЗЪ ТЕАТРИКА ПОЯВЛЯЕТСЯ СТАРЫЙ ФОКУСНИКЪ.
At the Front of [i.e., from inside] the Little Theater Appears the Old Magician.

ФОКУСЪ.   THE MAGIC TRICK.

ФОКУСНИКЪ ИГРАЕТЪ НА ФЛЕЙТѢ   The Magician Plays the Flute.

42

ЗАНАВѢСЪ ТЕАТРИКА РАЗДВИГАЕТСЯ; ТОЛПА ВИДИТЪ ТРИ КУКЛЫ: ПЕТРУШКУ, АРАПА И БАЛЕРИНУ.

The Curtain of the Little Theater Opens and the Crowd Sees Three Puppets: Petrushka (Guignol), a Moor, and a Ballerina.

ФОКУСНИКЪ ОЖИВЛЯЕТЪ ИХЪ ПРИ -
КОСНОВЕНІЕМЪ СВОЕЙ ФЛЕЙТЫ.
The Magician Brings Them to Life by Touching
Them Lightly with His Flute.

РУССКАЯ   RUSSIAN DANCE.

ПЕТРУШКА, АРАПЪ И БАЛЕРИНА ДРУЖНО ПУСКАЮТСЯ ВЪ ПЛЯСЪ КЪ ВЕЛИКОМУ УДИВЛЕНІЮ ВСѢХЪ.
Petrushka, the Moor, and the Ballerina Suddenly Begin to Dance, to the Great Astonishment of the Crowd.

*) Distant but violent sound. Adjust to the acoustics of the hall.

КАРТІНА ВТОРАЯ.
У ПЕТРУШКИ.

SECOND TABLEAU
Petrushka's Room.

ПРИ ПОДНЯТІИ ЗАНАВѢСА ДВЕРЬ ВЪ КОМНАТКѢ У ПЕТРУШКИ ВНЕЗАПНО ОТВОРЯЕТСЯ; ЧЬЯ-ТО НОГА ГРУБО ЕГО ВЫТАЛКИВАЕТЪ; ПЕТРУШКА ВАЛИТСЯ. ДВЕРЬ ЗА НИМЪ ЗАТВОРЯЕТСЯ.

As the Curtain Rises, the Door to Petrushka's Room Opens Suddenly; a Foot Kicks Him Onstage; Petrushka Falls and the Door Closes Again Behind Him.

48 *) In concert performance this drumroll is omitted.

60 ОТЧАЯНИЕ ПЕТРУШКИ.
Petrushka's Despair.

КАРТИНА ТРЕТЬЯ.
У АРАПА.

THIRD TABLEAU
The Moor's Room.

ТАНЕЦЪ БАЛЕРИНЫ.
(СЪ КОРНЕТЪ-А-ПИСТОНОМЪ ВЪ РУКАХЪ).

DANCE OF THE BALLERINA
(Cornet in Hand).

ВАЛЬСЪ.
(БАЛЕРИНА И АРАПЪ.)

WALTZ
(The Ballerina and the Moor).

АРАПЪ И БАЛЕРИНА ПРИСЛУЩИВАЮТСЯ.
The Moor and the Ballerina Prick Up Their Ears.

ПОЯВЛЕНІЕ ПЕТРУШКИ.
Appearance of Petrushka.

ССОРА АРАПА СЪ ПЕТРУШКОЙ. БАЛЕРИНА ПАДАЕТЪ ВЪ ОБМОРОКЪ.

The Fight Between the Moor and Petrushka. The Ballerina Faints.

КАРТИНА ЧЕТВЕРТАЯ.
НАРОДНЫЯ ГУЛЯНІЯ НА МАСЛЕНОЙ.
(ПОДЪ ВЕЧЕРЪ.)

FOURTH TABLEAU
The Shrovetide Fair (Toward Evening).

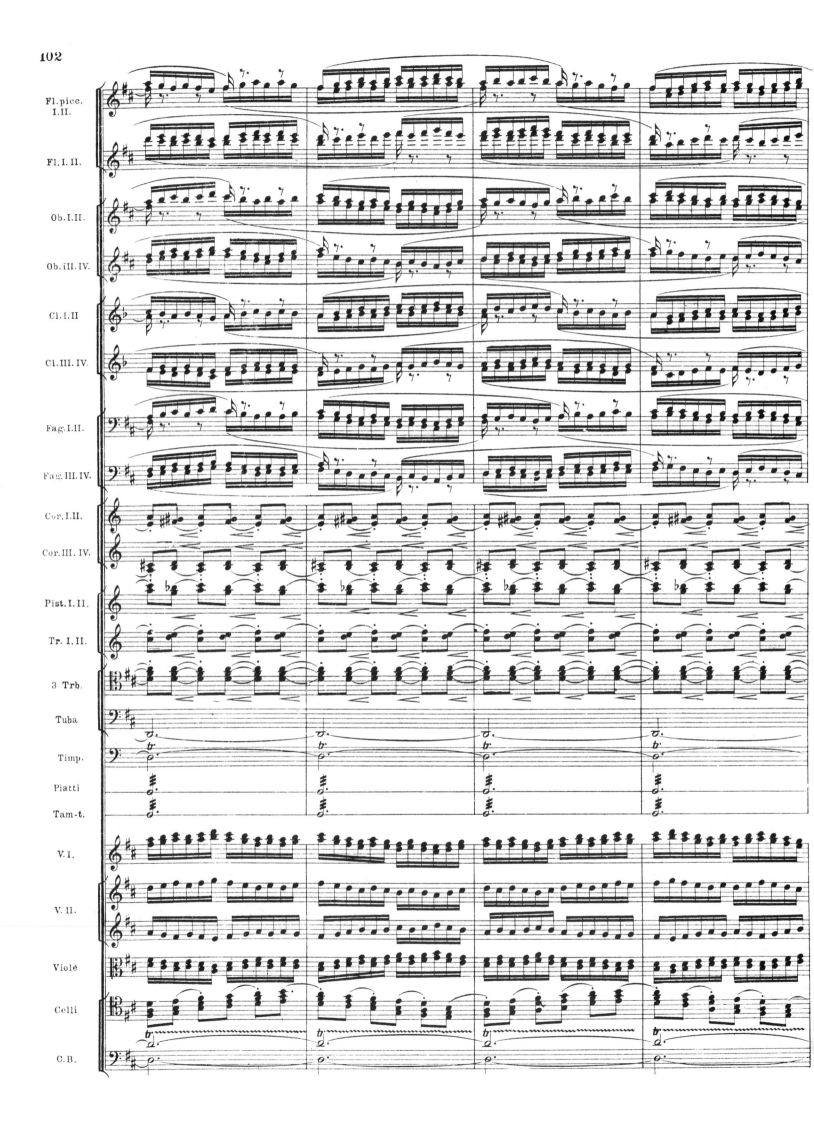

ТАНЕЦЪ КОРМИЛИЦЪ.   THE WET-NURSES' DANCE.

ВХОДИТЪ МУЖИКЪ СЪ МЕДВѢДЕМЪ. ВСѢ. КИДАЮТСЯ ВЪ СТОРОНУ.

A Peasant Enters with a Bear. Everyone Scatters.

МУЖИКЪ ИГРАЕТЪ НА ДУДКѢ — МЕДВѢДЬ ХОДИТЪ НА ЗАДНИХЪ ЛАПАХЪ.
The Peasant Plays the Pipe. The Bear Walks on His Hind Feet.

МУЖИКЪ СЪ МЕДВѢДЕМЪ УДАЛЯЮТСЯ.
The Peasant and the Bear Leave.

118

КИПЫ АССИГНАЦІИ.

103 ЦЫГАНКИ ТАНЦУЮТЪ. КУПЕЦЪ ИГРАЕТЪ НА ГАРМОНИКѢ
The Gypsy Women Dance. The Merchant Plays the Accordion.

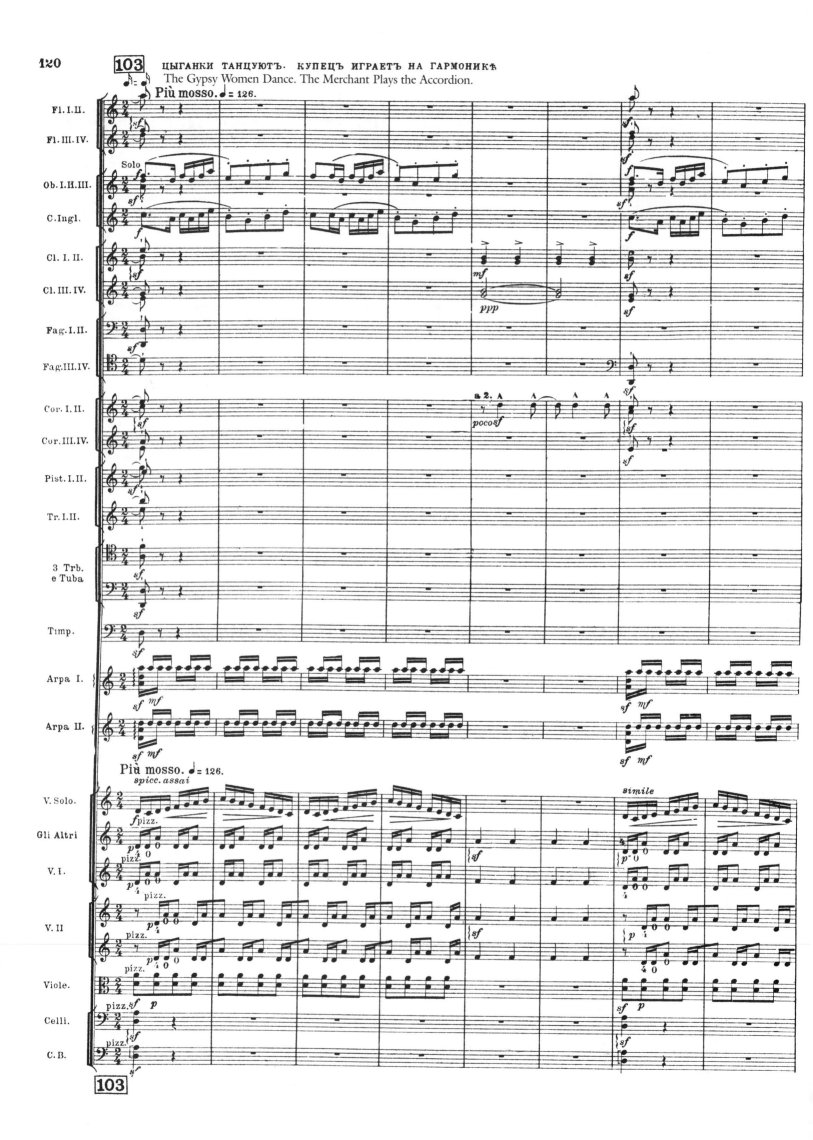

*) come sopra (sempre)

107 КУПЕЦЪ И ЦЫГАНКИ УДАЛЯЮТСЯ.
The Merchant and the Gypsies Leave.

ТАНЕЦЪ КУЧЕРОВЪ И КОНЮХОВЪ.   DANCE OF THE COACHMEN AND THE GROOMS.

КОРМИЛИЦЫ ТАНЦУЮТЪ ВМѢСТѢ СЪ КУЧЕРАМИ И КОНЮХАМИ.
The Wet-Nurses Dance with the Coachmen and the Grooms.

116
Fl. I. II.
Fl. III.
Fl. IV.
Ob. I. II.
Ob. III.
Ob. IV.
Cl. I. II.
Cl. III.
Cl. IV.
Fag. I. II.
Fag. III.
Fag. IV.
= Contrafagotto
Cor. I. II.
Cor. III. IV.
Pist. I. II.
Tr. I. II.
3 Trb. e Tuba.
Timp.
Gr. Cassa.
Arpe I. II. a 2.
V. I.
V. II.
Viole.
Celli.
C. B.
116

РЯЖЕНЫЕ. THE MUMMERS.

ЧОРТЪ (МАСКА) ЗАИГРЫВАЕТЪ СЪ ТОЛПОЙ. The Devil (Mummer) Induces the Crowd to Frolic with Him.

БАЛАГУРСТВО РЯЖЕНЫХЪ .(КОЗЫ СО СВИНЬЕЙ.)
Buffoonery of the Mummers (Goat and Pig).

МАСКИ И РЯЖЕНЫЕ ТАНЦУЮТЪ.
The Mummers and the Maskers Dance.

ОСТАЛЬНЫЕ ПРИСОЕДИНЯЮТСЯ КЪ ПЛЯСКѢ РЯЖЕНЫХЪ.
The Rest of the Crowd Joins in the Mummers' Dance.

ТОЛПА ПРОДОЛЖАЕТЪ ТАНЦОВАТЬ НЕ ОБРАЩАЯ НИКАКОГО ВНИМА-
НІЯ НА КРИКИ ДОНОСЯЩІЕСЯ ИЗЪ МАЛЕНЬКАГО ТЕАТРИКА.
The Crowd Continues to Dance Without Taking Notice of the Cries Com-
ing from the Little Theater.

The Dances Break Off. Petrushka Dashes from the Little Theater, Pursued by the Moor, Whom the Ballerina Tries to Restrain.

ОНЪ ЖАЛОБНО УМИРАЕТЪ.   ПОСЫЛАЮТЪ БУДОЧНИКА ЗА ФОКУСНИКОМЪ.
He Dies, Still Moaning. A Policeman Is Sent to Look for the Magician.

ПРИХОДИТЪ ФОКУСНИКЪ.   ОНЪ ПОДЫМАЕТЪ ТРУПЪ ПЕТРУШ-
The Magician Arrives.   He Picks up Petrushka's Corpse,

КИ И ТРЯСЕТЪ ЕГО.
Shaking It.

НАРОДЪ РАСХОДИТСЯ. The Crowd Disperses.

ФОКУСНИКЪ ОСТАЕТСЯ ОДИНЪ НА СЦЕНѢ. ОНЪ ТАЩИТЪ ТРУПЪ ПЕТРУШКИ ВЪ ТЕАТРИКЪ.
The Magician Remains Alone on the Stage. He Drags Petrushka's Corpse toward the Little Theater.

НАДЪ ТЕАТРИКОМЪ ПОЯВЛЯЕТСЯ ТѢНЬ ПЕТРУШКИ, ГРОЗЯЩЯЯ И ПОКАЗЫВАЮЩІАЯ ДЛИННЫЙ НОСЪ ФОКУСНИКУ.
Above the Little Theater Appears the Ghost of Petrushka, Menacing, Thumbing His Nose at the Magician.

ФОКУСНИКЪ ВЪ УЖАСѢ ВЫПУСКАЕТЪ ИЗЪ РУКЪ КУКЛУ-ПЕТРУШКУ И,
БОЯЗЛИВО ОЗИРАЯСЬ, ПОСПѢШНО УХОДИТЪ.
The Terrified Magician Lets the Puppet-Petrushka Drop from His Hands and Exits Quickly,
Casting Frightened Glances over His Shoulder.

ЗАНАВѢСЪ.
Curtain.

L'istesso tempo.   Molto più lento.

L'istesso tempo.   Molto più lento.

Fin.

ROME 13/26 MAI 1911.

Для концертнаго исполненія пользоваться вмѣсто стр. 150 этой стр. 150ª.

For concert performance, page 150a should be used in place of page 150.